Drawing Is Fun!

DRAWING MANGA

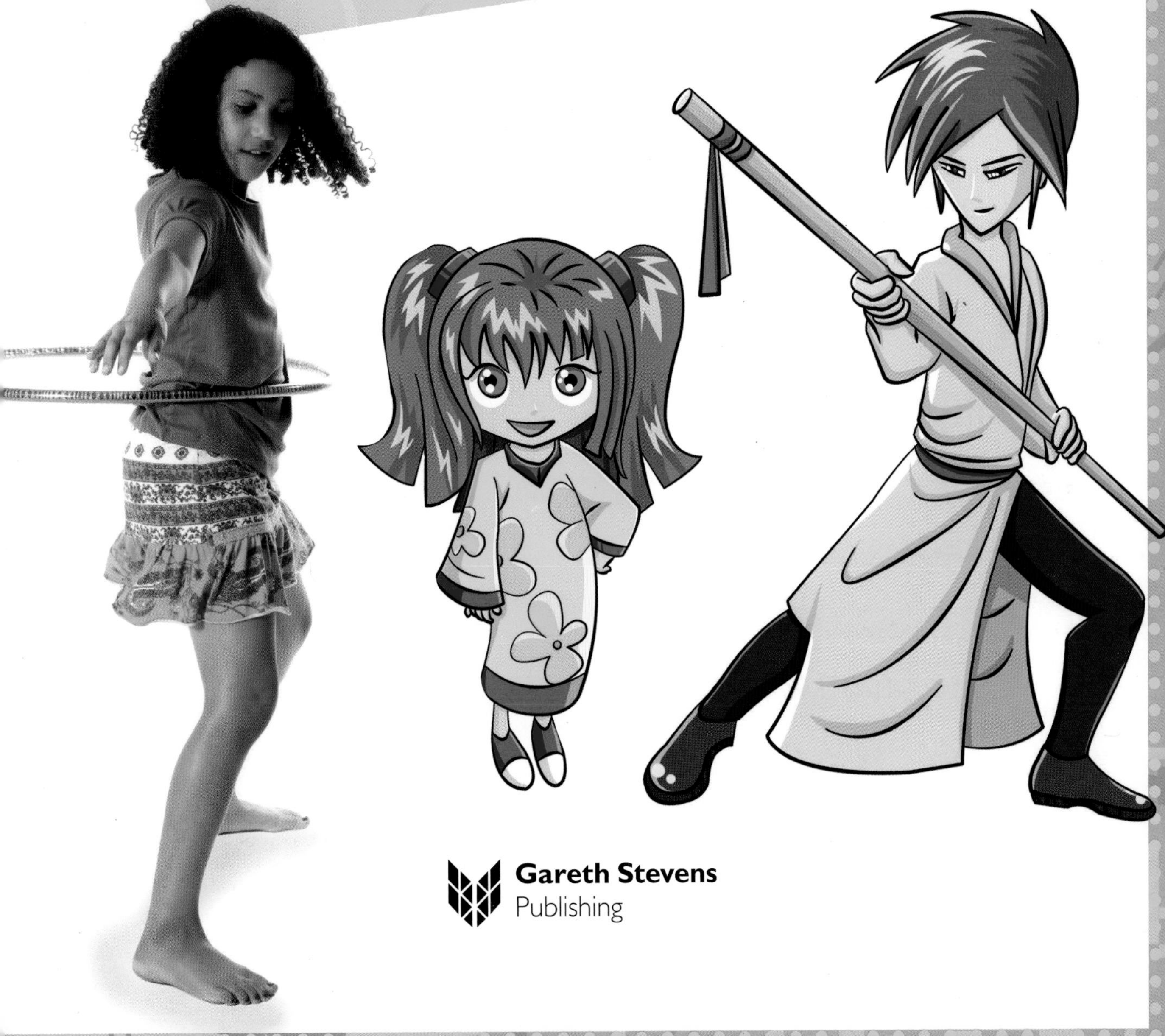

Gareth Stevens Publishing

Please visit our Web site, www.garethstevens.com. For a free color catalog of all our high-quality books, call toll free 1-800-542-2595 or fax 1-877-542-2596.

Library of Congress Cataloging-in-Publication Data

Cook, Trevor, 1948-
Drawing manga / Trevor Cook and Lisa Miles.
    p. cm. — (Drawing is fun!)
Includes index.
ISBN 978-1-4339-5067-4 (pbk.)
ISBN 978-1-4339-5068-1 (6-pack)
ISBN 978-1-4339-5024-7 (library binding)
1. Comic books, strips, etc.—Japan—Technique—Juvenile literature.
2. Cartooning—Technique—Juvenile literature. I. Miles, Lisa. II. Title.
NC1764.5.J3C65 2011
741.5'1—dc22
                                    2010027759
First Edition

Published in 2011 by
Gareth Stevens Publishing
111 East 14th Street, Suite 349
New York, NY 10003

Artwork: Q2A India
Text: Trevor Cook and Lisa Miles
Editors: Fiona Tulloch and Joe Harris
Cover design: Akihiro Nakayama

Picture credits: All photographs supplied by iStockphoto; except for pages 4, 6 and 30, supplied by Shutterstock; and page 28, supplied by Alamy.

Printed in the United States

CPSIA compliance information: Batch #AW11GS: For further information contact Gareth Stevens, New York, New York at 1-800-542-2595.

SL001679US

Contents

Cute manga girl

Manga is the Japanese word for comic books. It is also a way of drawing.

Let's turn this girl into a manga drawing!

She stands in a cute way. She has her hand on her hip. Her eyes are wide open.

She is wearing a pretty dress and matching shoes.

FUN FACTS ● FUN FACTS ● FUN FACTS ● FUN FACTS ● FUN FACTS

Manga began in Japan more than 50 years ago. Now it is popular all over the world!

1. Start with her head and body.

2. Put in some long hair...

3. ... and some more long hair.

4. She's wearing a pretty yellow dress.

Skateboarder

Manga stories are full of action. This skateboarder would make a great manga figure.

He has messy hair.

His skateboard has four wheels.

He wears baggy clothes. They let him move easily.

FUN FACTS ● FUN FACTS ● FUN FACTS ● FUN FACTS ● FUN FACTS

A skater can make the board jump into the air using only his feet. This famous trick is called an "ollie."

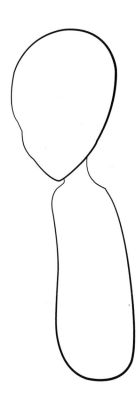

1. Begin with his head and body.

2. Make his hair a bit messy.

3. He's carrying a skateboard.

4. Finish off with his legs.

Girl and cat

Here is another cute picture. Manga figures are often cute.

This girl loves her cat. It's friendly and fun to play with.

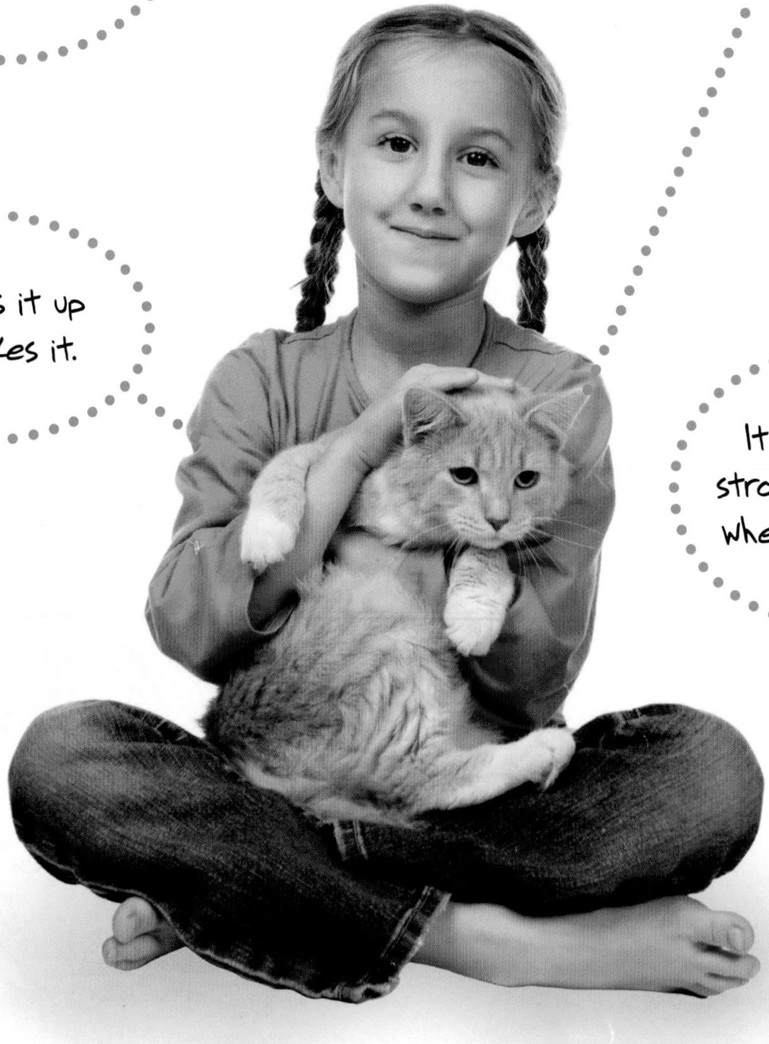

She picks it up and strokes it.

It likes being stroked. It purrs when it's happy.

FUN FACTS ● FUN FACTS ● FUN FACTS ● FUN FACTS ● FUN FACTS

Some manga stories are about animals that act like people. A famous manga movie is called "The Cat Returns."

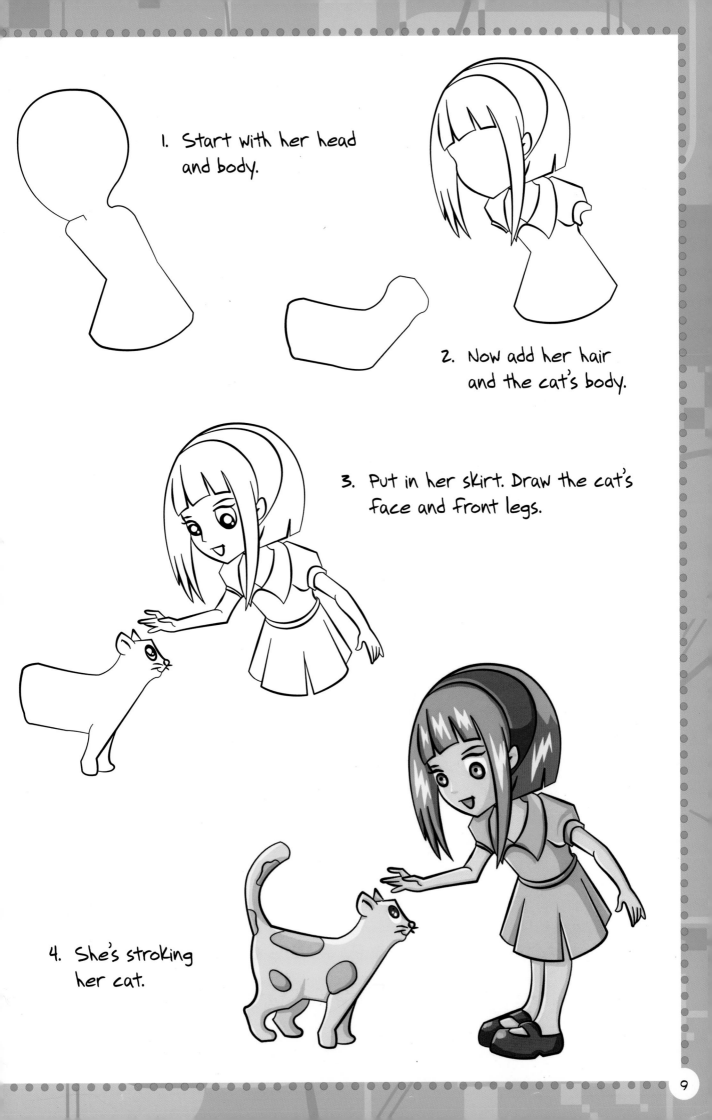

1. Start with her head and body.

2. Now add her hair and the cat's body.

3. Put in her skirt. Draw the cat's face and front legs.

4. She's stroking her cat.

Karate fighter

Karate is a sport from Japan. In Karate, two people fight against each other.

This fighter hits and kicks to score points.

She has to be strong and quick to fight well.

Her belt is orange. It shows that she is no longer a beginner.

FUN FACTS ● FUN FACTS ● FUN FACTS ● FUN FACTS ● FUN FACTS

A white belt shows that the fighter is a beginner. A black belt shows that the fighter is an expert.

1. Draw her head and body.

2. Her face is angry.

3. Draw the long ponytail.

4. She's punching the air!

Hula hoop girl

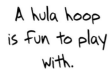

A hula hoop is fun to play with.

This girl makes her body go round in circles. This makes the hula hoop spin.

To keep it spinning, she has to move really fast.

Sometimes, people spin several hula hoops at the same time.

FUN FACTS ● FUN FACTS ● FUN FACTS ● FUN FACTS ● FUN FACTS

People try to spin the hula hoop for as long as they can. The longest spin ever lasted over three and a half days!

1. Here's her head and body.

2. Put in her hair and arms.

3. Add her face.

4. She's playing with hoops.

Girl in the rain

She has an umbrella. It keeps the rain off her.

This girl wears a raincoat to keep her dry.

She wears boots for splashing in the puddles.

Walking in the rain is fun if you wear the right clothes!

FUN FACTS ● FUN FACTS ● FUN FACTS ● FUN FACTS ● FUN FACTS

The first umbrellas were used to protect people from the sun, not the rain.

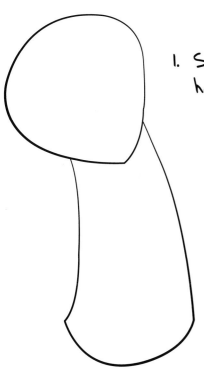

1. Start with her head and body.

2. Now put on her hair and a coat.

3. She has a hat...

4. ... and a colorful umbrella.

Jumping rope

Jumping rope is great exercise. It keeps you fit!

The boy jumps rope forward. He brings the rope over his head from the back.

He can jump rope on the spot. Or he can run and jump rope at the same time.

He can also jump rope backward. He brings the rope over from the front.

FUN FACTS ● FUN FACTS ● FUN FACTS ● FUN FACTS ● FUN FACTS

In 1995, a man ran a marathon race while jumping rope all the way!

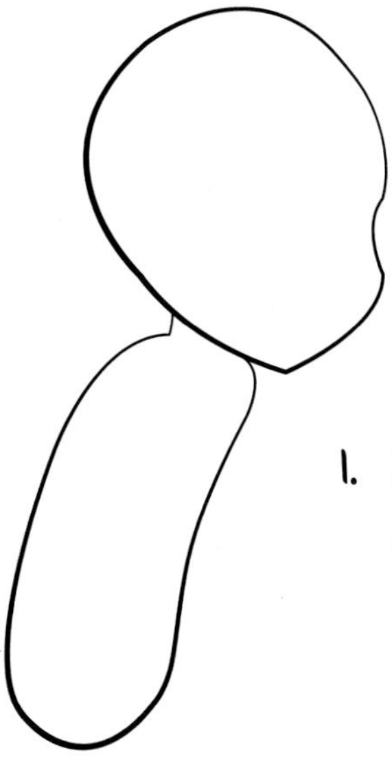

1. Draw the head and body.

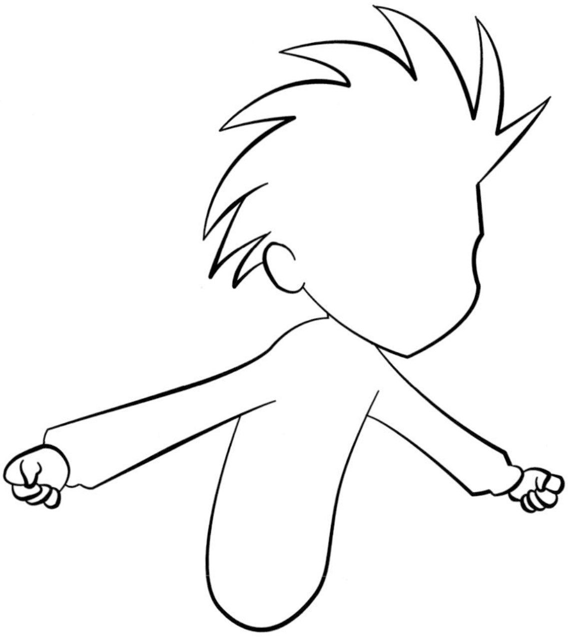

2. In manga drawings, people often have spiky hair.

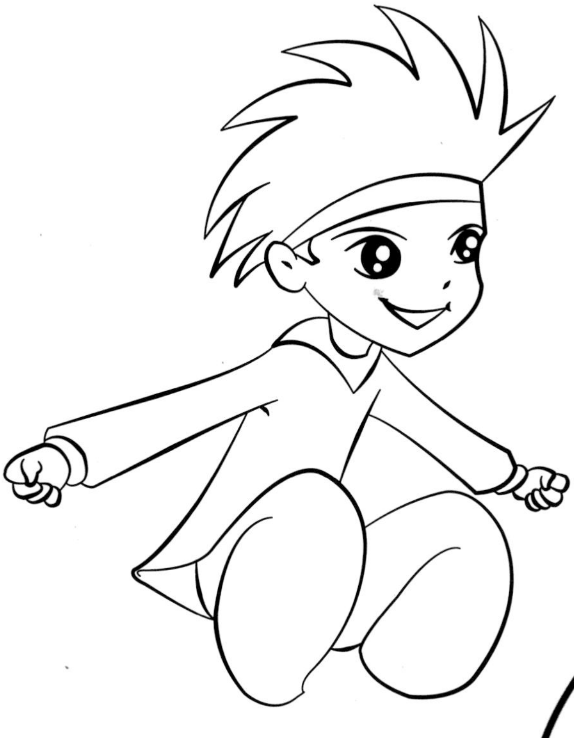

3. Put in the arms and legs.

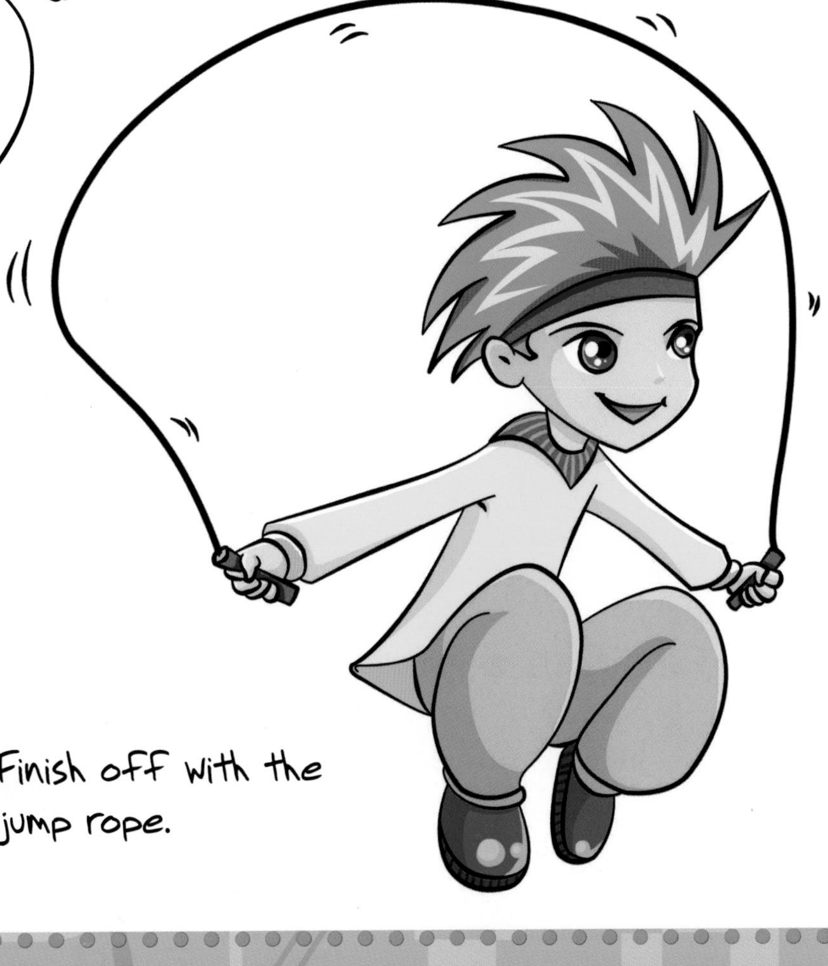

4. Finish off with the jump rope.

Boy with sword

Fighting sports are called martial arts.

This boy is practicing martial arts moves with a toy sword.

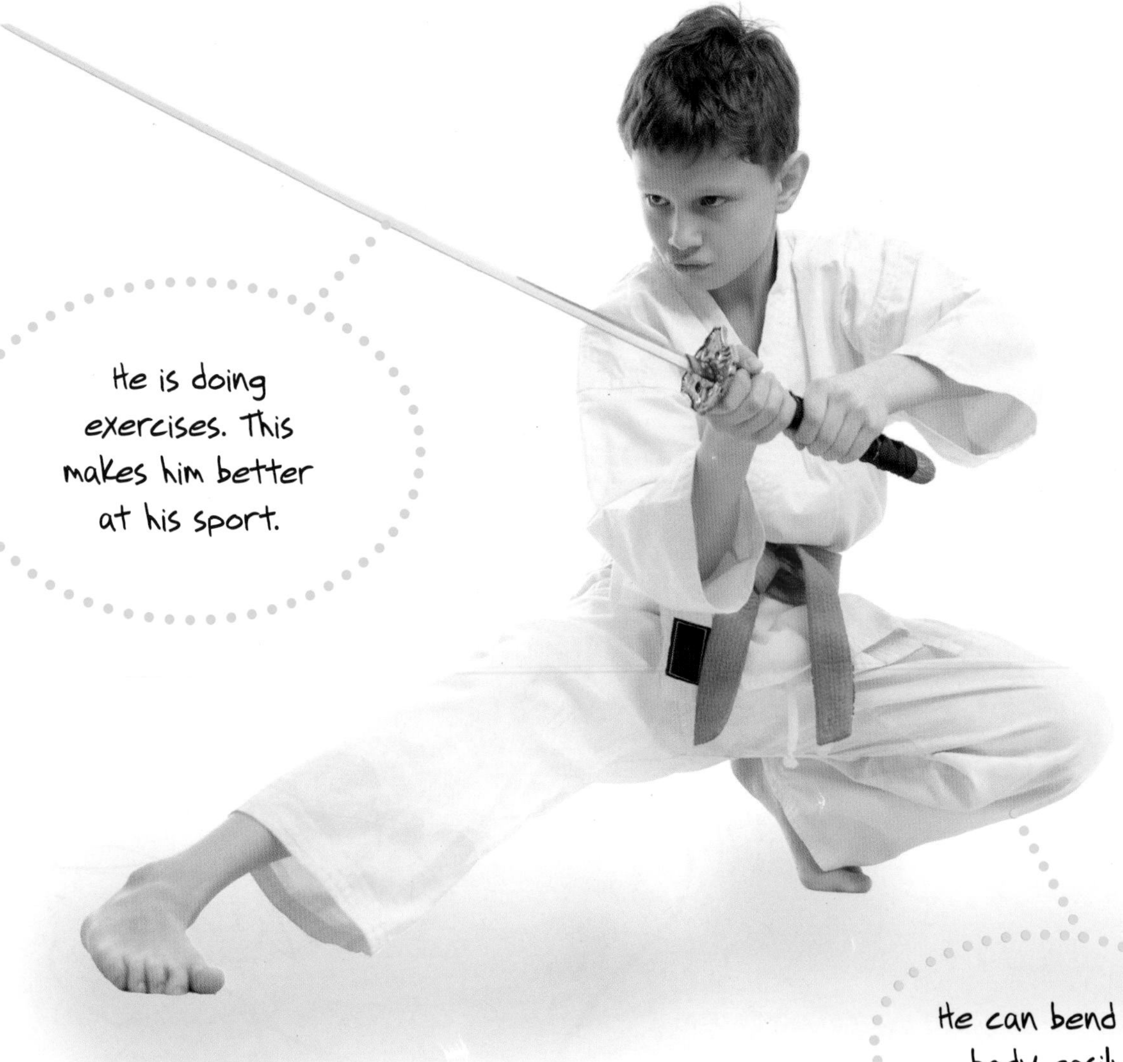

He is doing exercises. This makes him better at his sport.

He can bend his body easily.

FUN FACTS ● FUN FACTS ● FUN FACTS ● FUN FACTS ● FUN FACTS

In a Japanese sport called "kendo," people fight with swords. The fighters wear body armor!

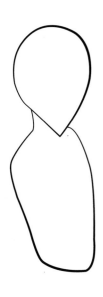

1. Here's his head and body.

2. Put in his arms.

3. Add lots of hair and the hands.

4. He has a sword.

Baseball player

This baseball player wears a cap to keep the sun out of her eyes.

She swings the baseball bat at the ball to hit it.

The ball is very hard. It can go a long way if it is hit well.

FUN FACTS ● FUN FACTS ● FUN FACTS ● FUN FACTS ● FUN FACTS

People in Japan love baseball. There are many manga stories about baseball.

1. Begin with her head and body.

2. She's wearing a hat.

3. Add a skirt and her arms.

4. Put in her legs and a bat.

Karate Kicker

There are lots of ways to kick in Karate. It takes a lot of practice!

This fighter is doing a high kick.

He kicks with this leg. He keeps it very straight.

He jumps high into the air to do the kick.

FUN FACTS ● FUN FACTS ● FUN FACTS ● FUN FACTS ● FUN FACTS

Karate is a Japanese word. It means "empty hand."

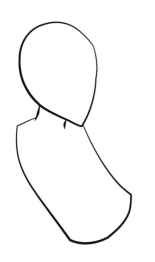

1. Draw his body and head.

2. Now add his arms.

3. Put in his face.

4. Now the legs.
   He's kicking out.

Girl with staff

This girl is doing a martial art.

She tries to push another fighter over with her staff.

She's using a long stick called called a staff.

She uses the staff to stop being hit.

FUN FACTS ● FUN FACTS ● FUN FACTS ● FUN FACTS ● FUN FACTS

The staff is also called a "bo". This is a Japanese word.

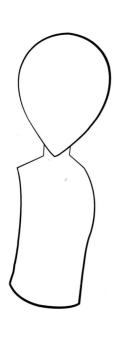

1. Start with her head and body.

2. Now add her hair and face.

3. Put in her long robe.

4. She's holding a staff.

Boy with staff

This boy is doing exercises.

The exercise is called a "kata."

He has to think hard to do the exercise.

He does the exercise over and over. This makes him stronger and faster.

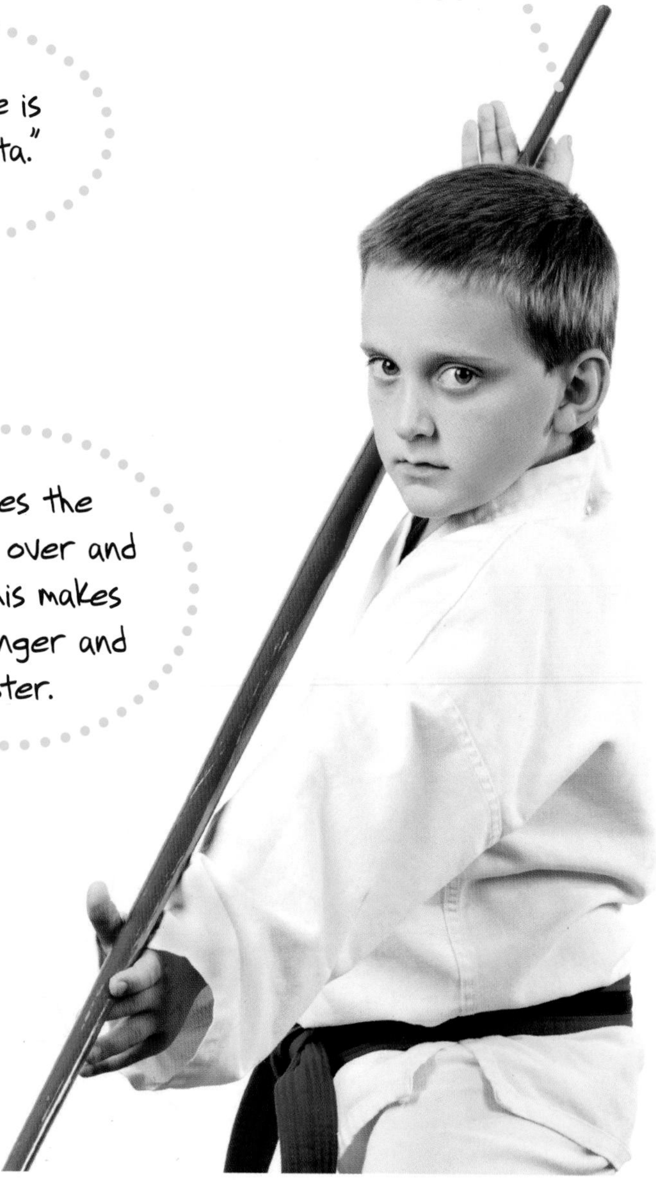

FUN FACTS ● FUN FACTS ● FUN FACTS ● FUN FACTS ● FUN FACTS

All sorts of weapons are used in martial arts. Sometimes people even use fans!

1. Begin with the head and body.

2. He looks quite cross.

3. Draw his arms next.

4. He has a long staff.

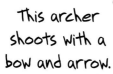

Archer

This archer shoots with a bow and arrow.

She aims carefully.

She pulls back the string to shoot the arrow.

The arrow flies fast through the air.

FUN FACTS ● FUN FACTS ● FUN FACTS ● FUN FACTS ● FUN FACTS

An arrow flies through the air very fast. It travels about twice as fast as a car on a highway!

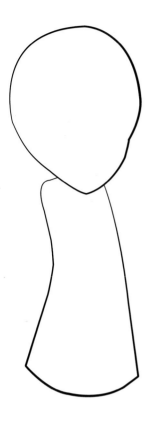

1. Start with her head and body.

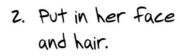

2. Put in her face and hair.

3. Add her clothes and arms.

4. She has a bow and arrows.

Runner

This boy is running fast.

He wears shorts and a T-shirt. These let his arms and legs move easily.

He uses his arms to help him run.

He runs in bare feet. However top runners wear running shoes.

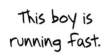

FUN FACTS ● FUN FACTS ● FUN FACTS ● FUN FACTS ● FUN FACTS

The fastest men on Earth run 100 yards in less than ten seconds. That's fast!

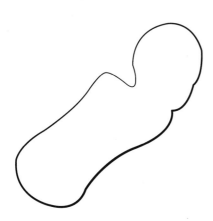

1. Draw the head and body.

2. Put in his hair and his shirt.

3. Now add his face and his running legs.

4. Finish off with his arms and feet.

Glossary

archer someone who uses a bow

arrow a pointed rod that is shot from a bow

baggy hanging in a loose way

baseball a ball game in which you hit a ball with a bat

comic book a book with pictures and speech bubbles. Some comic books are about superheroes.

expert someone who knows a lot about something, or who is really good at something

highway a fast road between cities. Highways have many lanes.

hip the place where your leg joins your body

Japan a country in the Far East

karate a martial art from Japan

manga a kind of comic art from Japan

marathon a long run. Most marathons are 26 miles long.

martial art a sport where you learn to fight

puddle a small pool of water

skateboard a board with four wheels on it

sword a sharp weapon

umbrella something that you hold to stop the rain from falling on you

weapon a tool for fighting

Index

Further Reading

Amberlyn, J.C. *Drawing Manga Animals, Chibis, and Other Adorable Creatures*. Watson-Guptill, 2009.

Camara, Sergi. *Art of Drawing Manga*. Sterling, 2007.

Hart, Christopher. *Manga for the Beginner*. Watson-Guptil, 2008.